The *Contemporary*
Hand Drummer

by José Rosa & Héctor "Pocho" Neciosup

Developing Contemporary Hand Drumming Techniques, Extraordinary Speed & Independence for the Contemporary Percussionist

ISBN: 978-1-57424-243-0
SAN 683-8022

Cover by Design Associates

Table of Contents
and 🔘 Track List

Table of Contents
and 〇 Track List

Foreword

The *Contemporary Hand Drummer* is a welcome addition to the canon of Afro-Caribbean hand drum method books. Hector and Jose have created a book that clearly explains the foundations of Afro-Caribbean music, including an excellent presentation of the clave concept, and a comprehensive chapter containing the patterns of many of the most popular rhythms. Several of the most important figures in the traditions and development of Afro-Caribbean hand drumming are included in this text. The brief biographies that accompany each "master" percussionist aid the student in better understanding of the history and the journey of this very special art form. The sections on applying the rudiments and on independence training have applications beyond hand drumming and will make any one mastering this material a stronger musician and percussionist. As the expectations of what a percussionist should know and the number of instruments he or she is expected to perform on continues to grow, books like this one are heaven sent and all too rare. Clear instructions and logically sequenced, this is a book that will help all who use it experience the indescribable feeling one gets while playing Afro-Caribbean music. It is a gift that needs to be shared and Jose and Hector have done precisely that; shared the gift of this music, heritage, and performing techniques in a book with strong educational concepts. I, along with many of their students, appreciate their efforts and now you can too. I thank Jose and Hector for writing this book and for sharing with you and me their incredible knowledge of this wonderful music.

Jeffrey M. Moore
Professor of Music
Director of Percussion Studies
University of Central Florida
http://music.ucf.edu/moore

Picture courtesy of Yamaha Corp.

Preface

First and foremost, I would like to thank my Lord and Savior Jesus Christ for the new life that he had given me in him. I want to thank my beautiful wife Maria and my children Elizabeth and Isaac for supporting me in this endeavor. I want to thank my students and all of those who inspire me daily to keep growing as an individual and as a teacher. To Professor Jeff Moore from the University of Central Florida, thanks for all your help, support and for allowing our summer camp to be held there. Thanks to my dear friend and second father Professor Jose "Pepe" Torres for your guidance and counseling. To my home church "Calvary Assembly of God" in Winter Park, FL, Thank you for being such a great blessing to my family. I want to thank my friend Glen Caruba from Pearl Percussion for all the support and friendship. To Pocho, thanks for being my friend and brother;

God Bless you,

Jose "Miguel" Rosa

First of all, I would like to thank my Lord and Savior Jesus Christ for salvation and for helping me discover my natural and spiritual talents. He is the reason why I write these pages. Once I was discouraged with my music but He gave me a new awakening, since then the knowledge I will share with you is an inspiration from God. I would like to thank my dad Moises Neciosup (R.I.P.) for your influence and your support in all the aspects of my life, I miss you dad. At the same time, I would like to thank my wife Sandra for her continual support even before we were married. A very special thanks to my two daughters Stephanie and Sarah, they are my number one fans, after every presentation they come to the stage for a hug. I thank my students and all of those who inspire me daily to keep growing as an individual and as a teacher. I want to thank my uncle Alex Neciosup Acuña (Alex Acuña) for your inspiration and help. To my friend Jose Rosa, Thank you for your sincere friendship, you are like a brother to me and you have shown me the love of God with your life.

Blessings to all,

Hector "Pocho" Neciosup

About the Authors

Picture provided by Jose Rosa: http://www.myspace.com/josemrosa

Jose Rosa

Born and raised in Humacao, Puerto Rico, At age 10 he was accepted in to a Music only middle/high school, where he learned to read music with professor Jose "Tito" Rivera. At age 12, he started playing with Humacao Symphonic Band under the direction of Professor German Peña Plaza. With the Humacao Symphonic Band, Jose traveled to Venezuela, New York, Costa Rica, Virgin Islands and Dominican Republic.

At age 14, he started formal percussion lessons with Professor Jose "Pepe" Torres. Under Torres coaching, Jose performed with the Puerto Rico Symphony Orchestra and with a variety of local bands. At the age of 15, he performed with a jazz big band named "Taller Pueblo", which was under the direction of his cousin Mariano Rodriguez. At age 17 he was accepted into the Puerto Rico Conservatory of Music where he studied percussion with Professor Jose Alicea. Under Alicea's coaching, Jose played for the America youth symphony orchestra as Principal Percussionist.

Through the course of his life, Jose has had the opportunity to perform with renown artists such as "Trumpet Virtuoso" - Arturo Sandoval, "El Maestro" Tito Puente, Mike Orta, Bobby Cruz, "Steel Pan virtuoso" Liam Teague, Richie Ray, Bobby Cruz, Christian Recording Artist Marcos Barrientos, Danilo Montero, Ingrid Rosario and many others. He had also performed at the Disney's Animal Kingdom "Tarzan Rocks" and "The Village Beatniks" shows, at the Universal Studios Florida "The I Love Lucy tribute show!", "Rico Monaco and Sol Sons", "Michael Andrews & Swingerhead", he can also be seen on the show "The Making of Disney's Animal Kingdom" on the Travel Channel and on "Jazz Then and Now" on syndicated PBS. He can also be seen with his own groups "Tinya", his latin jazz band "Jose Rosa and Friends" and "Los Rumberos de El Nuevo Día", Jose currently resides in Orlando, Florida where he performs, does recordings, teaches music on a regular basis at High Note Academy and as a guest artist for several universities.

He has co-written many instructional books along with his long time friend Professor Hector "Pocho" Neciosup. Jose is a Pearl Corporation and Centerstream / Hal Leonard Corporation Artist, Visit our summer camp website: http://www. contemporarypercussion.com .

Héctor "Pocho" Neciosup

Born and raised in Lima, Peru. Hector comes from a well known family of musicians his grandfather Fernando Neciosup, his dad Moises Neciosup Acuña both distinguished music teachers in Peru. But the person that inspired him the most was his uncle, Alejandro Neciosup Acuña (Alex Acuña) world renowned percussionist. Hector was introduced to percussion instruments from a very early age and by age seven he had mastered the basic beats for those instruments .At age fifteen, Hector was accepted at the Conservatory of music in Lima Peru. At age eighteen, he moved to the United States and participated in a drum contest directed by the legendary Louis Bellson, in which he won the first place. Consequently, Hector was granted a full scholarship to study at the University of Miami with Professor Steve Bagby and Professor Steve Rucker. During that period he was part of the faculty as Latin Percussion Instructor for Miami Institute of Percussion, which was founded by Russ Miller.

Through the course of his life, Hector has had the opportunity to perform and tour with major recording artists such as "Trumpet Virtuoso" Arturo Sandoval, Paquito D'Rivera, Alex Acuna and The Unknowns, Justo Almario, Eva Ayllon, Michael Brecker, Mongo Santamaria, Bob James, Eddie Daniels, Tania Maria, Nestor Torres, Mike Orta and Willy Chirino. He has also performed with several Christian recording artists such as Richie Ray, Grupo Nueva Vida, Bobby Cruz, Tom Brooks, Don Moen, Ingrid Rosario, Ricardo Rodriguez and Danilo Montero.

Presently, he is currently working with founder member of Cuban legendary band "Irakere" Mr. Carlos Averhoff and had recorded on his latest album entitled: "Jazz 'ta Bueno" (Universal Music). In addition, Hector has been on faculty at Florida International University for the past 10 years. Presently, Hector is one of the most sought after music teacher and performer in Miami, FL. Hector is a Pearl Percussion and CenterStream/Hal Leonard Artist. Visit our summer camp website: http://www.contemporarypercussion.com

Introduction {Track 1}

During our years of performing and educating, we have learned that the key to developing a good sound on the hand drums is to use practical strengthening exercises coupled with lots of repetition to develop the speed, independence and control needed to become a good hand drummer. Therefore, our goal is to help you develop a good sound by incorporating strengthening exercises coupled with various techniques to develop your strength, speed, independence and control needed.

This book was written to provide quick and to the point lessons so that you can take it with you and use it as a reference guide wherever you are. We have included some practical exercises for the Tumbao that will help you increase the strength, lessons on how to apply Snare Drum rudiments on to the hand drums and have dedicated a large section dealing with speed and techniques to develop a good solo performance. We wanted to address the issues relevant to both beginners and professionals in a step-by-step format that would be easily understood by anyone who reads it that has a little knowledge of music.

Regardless of whether you are looking to develop more strength, more speed or soloing, this book answers many questions you might have in regards to technique and soloing. It is our hope to pass on the knowledge and experience we have gained over the years studying and playing professionally in a way that can easily be understood to inspire the next generation of hand drummers.

Jose Rosa & Hector "Pocho" Neciosup

Chapter 1

"Introduction to the Hand drum and basic sounds"

Chano Pozo

Born 1/7/1915, killed in a bar room fight in Harlem 12/2/48. Played with Charlie Parker, Dizzy Gillespie, Chico O'Farrill, Carlos "Patato" Valdes, Miguelito Valdez, and many others as well.

He got his start after moving to New York in 1947 when Mario Bauza got him to play with Dizzy Gillespie, an event that changed the course of American Jazz. Chano Pozo thereby played a major role in the founding of Latin-jazz which was essentially a mixture of bebop and Cuban folk music. He gained his musical background from AfroCuban religions. Among his features with Dizzy were "Cubana Be," "Cubana Bop," "Tin Tin Deo" and "Manteca" which was later a big hit with Eddie Palmieri and Cal Tjader. Pozo co-wrote "Tin Tin Deo" and "Manteca"

How should I practice?  {Track 2}

The following chapter will set the foundation for the rest of this book. We will begin with the basics. In order for this book to benefit you, you will need to schedule a time on a regular basis to practice these techniques. We have come up with a sample practice plan to help guide you along the way. However, it is up to you how you want to plan your lessons. The most important thing is to be consistent with your lessons.

When teaching, we have found that our most effective practice time is done over 2 hour increments per session. For this reason, we have setup our sample practice plan in 2 hour increments. However, this may not fit your schedule. Therefore, if you can only practice 1 hour a day, just reduce the time we are presenting by half. If you are able to only practice 30 minutes a day then reduce the time by 4, etc.

The important thing to remember is to consistently follow through with the lessons regularly. When practicing we like to use a towel on the conga drum to warm up and to practice doubles. Why a towel? Because, it actually mutes the sound on the conga drum and it allows you to hear what you are doing easier. Not to mention the fact that it allows you to practice at any time during the day or night without disturbing others. Let's move on and look at **Jose and Pocho's 2 hours Daily practice plan**.

Jose and Pocho's 2 hours daily practice plan

1st ½ (Half) Hour

(Place a towel on the conga drum,
during the first 30 minutes only)

"Palm / Tip" Exercises – 10 Minutes
"Rudiment" Exercises – 10 Minutes
"Doubles and Mano Secreta" Exercises – 10 Minutes

While practicing doubles listen to the conga for articulation
on the bouncing. It is a good idea to have a mirror and of
course you should always have a metronome starting at
60 beats per minute.

2nd ½ (Half) Hour

(Remove towel from the conga drum)

"Open tones" - 5 Minutes
"Bass Tone" – 5 Minutes
"Tumbao" Exercises – 5 Minutes
"Tumbao" Exercise for Independence – 5 Minutes
Rhythms – *Mambo, Songo, Mozambique*, etc... – 10 Minutes

2nd Full Hour

"Marcha" and *"Soloing"* (Use our Play-along, if available) – 30 Minutes
Play-along with recordings – 30 Minutes

When practicing *"Tumbao exercises"*, listen to yourself and do the adjustments necessary until you are able to listen to a clean and "round sound" on the hand drums. When practicing the *Tumbao* exercises make sure to alternate hands. For example if you are right handed, switch to do the *Tumbao* with the Left hand and vice-versa.

During the play along time, we suggest that you spend that time playing along recordings and learning songs and solos. For best results we recommend that you use the accompanying play along which goes hand to hand with this book and it will help you develop more on the soloing area. Now that you have all the tools, let's begin with what we like to refer to as the *"Mazacote"*.

You can do your own schedule for any instrument, not necessarily the conga drums. This is just a sample guide, use your creativity and create your own. Let's move on and talk about how to care for your hands.

How to care for your hands

In recent times many people have asked us regarding this topic, that's why we decided to write in this regards. Good Diet, exercises, making sure to be hitting the drum properly and vitamin E cream in your hands before performing. In hand drumming your hands will always suffer, you will develop callous, your hand will bleed, will get swollen, you will even bleed through your urine. There is nothing we can do about that, because your hand needs to get stronger to be able to develop the proper sound for the hand drum. But we can care of our hands properly to minimize the damage.

A couple of years ago discussing about this issue with our friend Jose Gregorio Hernandez (Nestor Torres), he suggested the use of vitamin E prior to performance. We started using it and we noticed that the damage is minimized when the vitamin E is present in the hand. We'll recommend the Vitamin E that is sold at GNC, it is non-greasy and it doesn't stick the drum head. Let's move on to our next topic: "The Clave".

Let's talk about Clave

What is *"Clave"*? What does *"Clave"* means? How many types of *"Claves"* exist? According to the Spanish Dictionary the word *"Clave"* means "Key" but in reality, the term *"Clave"* refers to a 5-note rhythm pattern which is either played or implied in many types of Latin music. We usually compare the clave with the "pulse" used in Rock and in Jazz (2 & 4 pulse).

The five notes can be spaced in at least a half a dozen ways, but the whole pattern always lasts exactly four beats, although it's frequently written in the space of 8 beats. When a person comes to us to learn percussion and has no prior knowledge of music, the first thing we teach them is the *"Clave"*. Typically, we teach them the clave and many rhythms using the syllables. To learn clave we use the syllables *"TA"* for the clave accent and *"SH"* for the silence or where you are not supposed to play. Eventually, we ask them to mention *"TA"* only and the *"SH"* Part of it to sing in their minds.

3:2 Son Clave

One of the most common *claves* used in Latin music, is typically used in Son Montuno, Guaracha, Cha-cha-cha and many others. Traditionally is written as follows:

Ta, Sh Sh, Ta, Sh Sh, Ta, Sh Sh Sh, Ta, Sh, Ta, Sh Sh Sh

3:2 Rumba Clave  {Track 5}

Rumba clave is used in the majority of the Cuban music genres with the exception of the *Son, Son Montuno and Cha-cha-cha*. You can hear this *clave* used most widely in the "Guaguanco". The difference between *Rumba clave* and *Son clave* is that the third beat is played "late". Let's take a look at this example:

Ta, Sh Sh, Ta, Sh Sh Sh, Ta, Sh Sh, Ta, sh, Ta, Sh Sh Sh

We have discussed the *3:2 Son Clave* and *Rumba clave* and its difference. Its time to invert them and talk about the *2:3 Son and Rumba clave*.

Let's start with the 2:3 Son Clave.

2:3 Son Clave  {Track 6}

2:3 Son Clave is used in most modern Salsa arrangements and it starts with the second part of the *3:2 Clave*. Use the same technique that we explained before to learn this *clave*. Let's take a look at an example of this:

Sh Sh, Ta, sh, Ta, Sh Sh Sh   Ta, Sh Sh, Ta, Sh Sh, Ta, sh

2:3 Rumba Clave  {Track 7}

2:3 Rumba Clave, Let's take a look at an example of this:

Sh Sh, Ta, sh, Ta, Sh Sh Sh   Ta, Sh Sh, Ta, Sh Sh, sh, Ta

Hand Drum Tuning

How should I tune the Hand Drums?

There are many different ways to tune up Hand Drums, however we will share with you the way we tune them up. First of all, we would like to make sure that you understand where the middle C note is located on the piano or keyboard, is very close to the middle of the piano, also called C4; is carries this name because is the fourth C you find on the piano, starting from left to right, and this is a good starting point. When we use two congas, we use a "*Quinto*" and a "*Tumba*". We tune the "*Quinto*" on C4 and the "*Tumba*" on G3, which is the fourth white note before C4 to the left.

When we use three congas; we add a *"Conga"* and we tune it on Bb3, which is the black key just before C4.

If we use four congas, we add the E3 which is the sixth white note before C4 to the left for "Salsa" music.

Sometimes during recording sessions we tune up the set of congas according to the key of the song being played, this creates a unity with the band. Another way to think about the tuning could be, think of "Here Comes the Bride" melody; the *tumba* will play the first note while the quinto the next three notes and this will become your starting point.

Another way to think about it is, play the *Guaguanco* rhythm and listen how the open sounds, sound like. "*Kum - quin-quin – kum*". The "*Kum*" sound is for the tumba while the "*quin*" sound for the *quinto*. You can also use this as your starting point.

Let's talk about how to tune the congas for a "*Pop music ensemble*". We use the same method as above with the following guidelines. If we have 2 congas, tune the "*Tumba*" in G3 and the "*Quinto*" in C4, the third conga should be tuned in Bb3 but the fourth conga should be tuned in Eb4 instead of E3 as shown above, with 4 congas you should have a C minor Flat 7 chord.

We always recommend our students to first learn the notes on the piano and then memorize how they sound. For percussionist, we always recommend that you take piano lessons; because it will help you develop your musical ear and it will also help you understand more the music you are performing.

Let's talk about the Bongo Drums, generally the macho head (Small Drum) is tuned very tight so you get a nice crisp open tone, this way martillo (most basic bongo rhythm) has a nice sharp "tic" to it. The hembra (Big Drum) will be tuned much lower in pitch then the macho. I know some players who like to keep the macho and hembra roughly an octave apart. If you're not sure how the bongo should sound, I suggest listening to some Salsa or Latin Jazz recordings. When you hear a bongo sound you like, try to match the sound with your own bongo.

In terms of tuning African Style Rope Tuned Djembes, The Tuning is accomplished by pulling the vertical laces together at a number of points. This effectively pulls the top ring and bottom ring together.

Since the bottom ring cannot move upward due to the taper on the drum shell, the top ring is pulled downward, thus pulling on the drumhead and tightening the skin. The vertical laces are pulled together by a process known as pulling diamonds. To pull a diamond, follow the instructions below:

1. Find the place where the last diamond was formed. (The extra lace will be coming from this point).

2. From this point look to the top ring and identify the next two adjacent laces to be used.

3. Pass the extra lace under these two vertical laces and then return to pass under the first vertical lace. *Note: The lacing on your drum has been left at this point.*

4. Pull hard on the extra lace and a diamond will form. A pull down towards the bottom will help keep the diamonds small and regular.

5. If one diamond is sufficient to tune your drum, form a simple knot by passing the extra lace under the diamond point and back through the loop formed, or you may wish to pull several diamonds and then tie it off."

Jose teaching the bongos.

Pocho teaching at camp.

How do I develop good sound on congas?
{Track 8}

We've often been asked been asked this question by both students and fellow conga players. Basically, how good of a conga sound you get relies on how and where you hit the conga drum. The conga drum has 2 hitting areas:

The open tone / Slap area

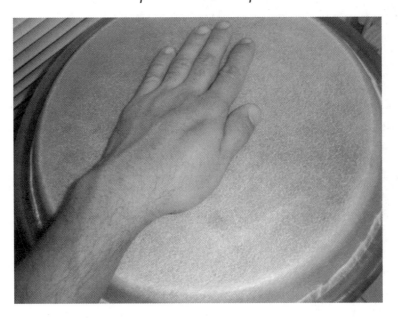

The Bass sound / "Baqueteo" area

In order to get a full rounded open tone on the congas you need to use 4 full fingers with the beginning of the palm inside the drum (as you see in the picture).

The following exercises work on developing the open tone and Bass sound on the congas. The more you practice this exercises the better you'll be; make sure to listen to yourself for a "rounded" sound or what we call in Spanish "Sonido Macho" (Male Sound).

Exercise (A)　{Track 9}

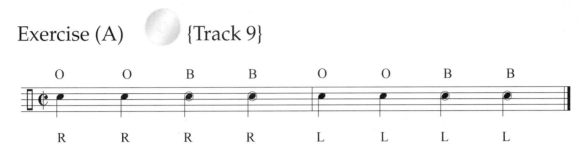

O	O	B	B	O	O	B	B
R	R	R	R	L	L	L	L

Exercise (B)

1-	R	L	R	L	R	L	R	L
2-	L	R	L	R	L	R	L	R
3-	R	R	L	R	L	L	R	L
4-	R	L	R	R	L	R	L	L
5-	R	R	R	L	L	L	L	R

Exercise (C)　{Track 10}

1-	R	L	R	L	R	L	R	L
2-	L	R	L	R	L	R	L	R
3-	R	R	L	R	L	L	R	L
4-	R	L	R	R	L	R	L	L
5-	R	R	R	L	L	L	L	R

Exercise (D)　{Track 11}

1-	R	L	R	L	R	L	R	L	R	L	R	L	R	L	R	L
2-	R	R	R	R	R	R	R	R	R	R	R	R	R	R	R	R

Exercise (E)

1-	L	R	L	R	L	R	L	R	L	R	L	R	L	R	L	R
2-	R	R	R	R	L	L	L	L	R	R	R	R	L	L	L	L
3-	R	R	L	L	R	R	L	L	R	R	L	L	R	R	L	L

Exercise (F)

| 1- | L | L | L | L | L | L | L | L | L | L | L | L | L | L | L | L |
| 2- | R | R | L | R | R | R | L | R | R | R | L | R | R | R | L | R |

Exercise (G)

| 1- | R | L | R | R | L | R | L | L | R | L | R | R | L | R | L | L |
| 2- | R | L | L | R | L | L | R | L | R | L | L | R | L | L | R | L |

16

Developing Palm / Tip Techniques

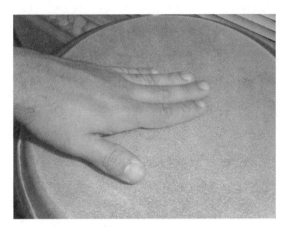

| Palm Technique | Finger Tip Technique |

Many people that we've known had asked us: *"How important is having a good "Baqueteo" (Palm/ tip technique)?"* In our opinion, developing a good Palm/Tip technique is very important because it creates stability in the *Tumbao*. Remember the *Palm/Tip* is responsible for keeping the *Tumbao* together and keeping the tempo. If you have a weak *"Baqueteo"* it will affect the band adversely. If you listen carefully to a "Salsa" band recording you will notice that the *"Baqueteo"* is pretty strong and it actually "marches" through the song. That's why we call the *Tumbao*, *"Marcha"* or *March*, because it guides the band and it also tightens the percussion section together.

There are many exercises you can use to develop a good *Palm/tip* technique but the following are just an example. These exercises can be practiced by using a table or the conga drum covered with a towel. Please remember to use a metronome when practicing these exercises, always starting on 60 beats per minute all the way up to 200 beats per minute. Remember to alternate your hands when practicing these exercises so your hand will be developing at the same time. On the next page you will see several exercises that we use with our students to help them develop the *"Palm / Tip Technique"*.

In the next page, there are some variations, please study this exercises with both hands. Start slow and progressively speed it up until you are comfortable with the speed. Make sure NOT to over play yourself.

Exercise (A)  {Track 13}

Exercise (B) {Track 14}

Exercise (C)

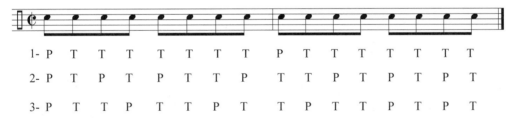

Exercise (D)

These are just few exercises; there are more exercises to develop the left hand located at the chapter entitled: *"La Mano Secreta"* at the end of the book. We recommend for you to practice these exercises on a daily basis. Let's move on…

How to develop a Good Open & Close Slap

This will be short and sweet. This is one of the most difficult sounds to develop. The way we look at it is as follows, first of all your hands must be relaxed. To create a good *"SLAP"* you must make some pressure on the head with your left hand (If you are left handed use your right hand) close to the center of the drum to muffle the head and with your right hand hit the area close to the Label.

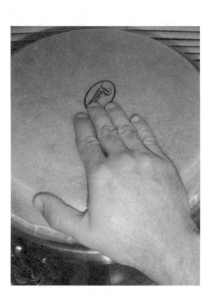

Left Hand   Right Hand

Remember you must master the close slap before working on the *open slap*. Consistency is very important at the time of developing the *slap*. The *close slap* must sound the same all the time. For an *open slap*, just direct yourself toward the center of the conga drum and hit the area where the "Logo" is located. By hitting the center of the drum you will notice that at first nothing will happen, but by practicing, eventually you will see the results.

Let's review and summarize the first 2 chapters of this book. We have learned how to develop a good *"open tone"*, a solid *"Palm/Tip"* technique, *Bass tone* and *open & close slap*. On the next page we want to give you some exercises using the first 4 sounds of the congas.

Exercises to develop sound

Exercise (A)   {Track 15}

Exercise (B)   {Track 16}

Exercise (C)   {Track 17}

Exercise (D)

Exercise (E)   {Track 18}

Exercise (F)

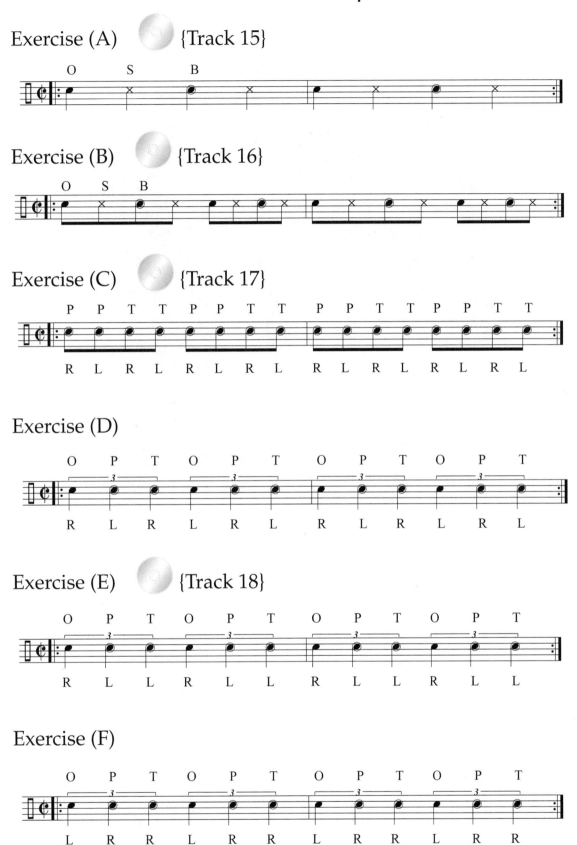

This will end this chapter; let's move on to "Developing the Tumbao and introduction to the contemporary tumbao".

Tata Guines

Tata Güines (born Federico Aristides Soto y Alejoà on June 30, 1930, in Güines, Matanzas province, Cuba - February 4, 2008 in Havana, Cuba) was a Cuban percussionist and composer.

Tata Guines was known as the "King of the Congas" and "Golden Hands". He had a musical career that lasted six decades that helped popularize Afro-Cuban rhythms.

"One of the most revolutionary performers in history, he was the first to perform using his nails and developed new techniques that are used today. Maestros de Maestros, mentor for Giovanni Hidalgo and many others. At one point considered the best conga player in the world until Giovanni Hidalgo took the title. Tata Guines will always live in our minds and souls, He'll be always considered the best there is, the best it was and the best it will be."

Carlos "Patato" Valdez

Carlos Valdes (November 4, 1926 – December 4, 2007) born in Cuba in 1926, living in New York City since 1954. Patato has played with Dizzy Gillespie, Art Blakey, Tito Puente, Machito, Mario Bauza, Quincy Jones and many other salsa and jazz stars. The first conguero to tune his congas to a song's dominant chord and the first one to use 2 and 3 tumbadoras to perform with a band. Patato's influence was felt on the jazz and Latin music scenes and also in the world of film, where he gave Brigitte Bardot a mambo lesson in And God Created Woman.

Patato's work was most recently collected in Six Degrees' The Legend Of Cuban Percussion, which featured Omar Sosa, John Santiago, Changuito, Orestes Vilato and other Cuban and African all-star performers. He invented and patented the tunable conga drum (earlier drums had nailed heads) which revolutionized use of the instrument, even though he was never properly compensated for it by the companies that used them. Conga drumming is what it is today mainly thanks to "Patato" Valdez and without his invention the percussion industry wouldn't be what it is today. Thank you Patato.

Chapter 2

"Developing the Tumbao and introduction to the contemporary Tumbao"

Developing a Good Tumbao

{Track 19}

We have discussed earlier that *Tumbao* and *Marcha* are the same thing. Now, let's talk about how to develop a *good tumbao*. As a *Conguero*, it's important to have a solid *Tumbao* to be able to "drive" the band. Many people will argue that the person that drives the band is the Timbal Player. Well, maybe but if you have a *Conguero* with a weak *tumbao* it is hard for the *Timbalero* to drive the band and vice-versa if you have a weak Timbalero the band will also suffer. That's why we believe that the *Conguero and the Timbalero* drives the band together and they are responsible for making the band sound *"tight"*.

That's why having a *good tumbao* will help the *Timbalero* to perform without worries and also helps the band to perform more relaxed. The left hand (for right handed and Right for left handed) on the *tumbao* must be solid; a weak left hand (or right hand) will lead to a poor performance and instability on the tempo.

Typically, when we practice the *tumbao* we divide them in 2 parts and practice them separately. To create independence and stability we practice them with a metronome and also switching hands.

For example we might do the first exercise right handed and then switch to the left hand. Make sure to listen to yourself for articulation and clarity. Let's take a look at the first part of the *tumbao*.

The first part of the "Tumbao" is played on the "3" part of the Clave. The following Key is used for all exercises: P=Palm, T= Tip, O= Open Tone, S= Slap

Please practice this exercises very slow and eventually speed up.

{Track 20}

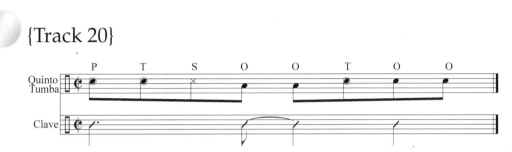

When practicing these exercises it's a very good idea to sing the part of the clave that is written. That way you become more familiar with the *tumbao* and you will know exactly where the *tumbao* goes with the clave. By the end of this chapter, we will put the *whole Tumbao* with the clave that way you can practice the *Tumbao* and sing the *clave* at the same time while playing.

{Track 21}

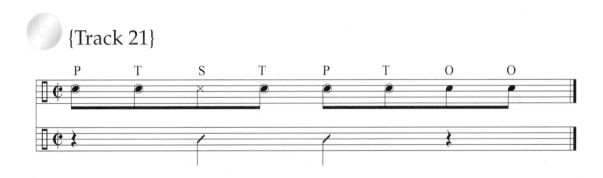

Now, let's take a look at the full *Tumbao* in both claves.

Let's start with the 3-2 Son Clave; we have provided you with a track to practice this exercise, it is very important to practice this exercise using the CD that is enclosed with this book, use the track where we show the 3-2 Son Clave. It will help you develop the *Tumbao*.

{Track 22}

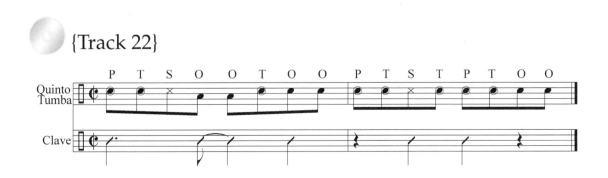

Pointer: It is a good idea to sing the clave while practicing this Tumbao, because it will create coordination and it will help you understand where everything goes. Now, let's take a look at the Tumbao with 2:3 clave, to practice this exercise use the track where we show the 2-3 Son Clave:

{Track 23}

Now that you understand how the *Tumbao* works let's take a look at some variations of the *Contemporary Tumbao for a contemporary Salsa band*. Enjoy…

Glen Caruba and Jose having fun at the Contemporary Drum and Percussion Summer camp while Pocho approves.

Contemporary Tumbao for 2 congas

We are including 3 basic variations of contemporary Tumbao that we used when performing with a contemporary Salsa Band.

{Track 24}

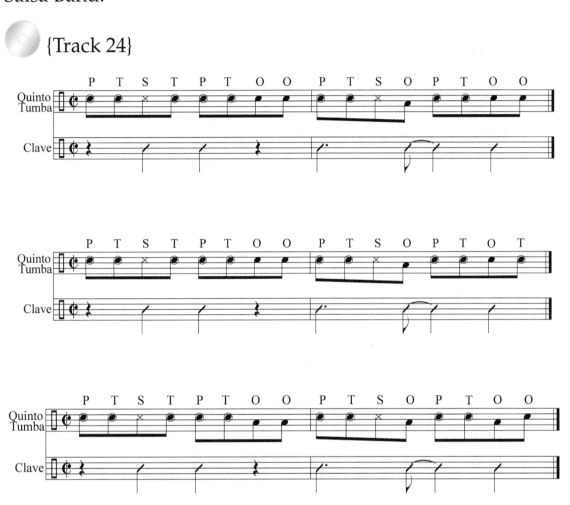

These are just some examples of a contemporary Tumbao, you can create your own version of tumbaos remember always to have respect of the founding rhythm and the clave. Let's take a look at the Bongo Drums, its history, basic sounds and contemporary rhythms.

The Bongo Drum

Bongo drums or bongos are a percussion instrument made up of two small drums attached to each other. The drums are of different size: the larger drum is called a *"hembra"* (Spanish: female), the smaller drum is called a *"macho"* (Spanish: male). Someone who plays the bongos is called a *"bongocero"*.

The *"Atlantic slave trade"* brought bongos to Cuba from Africa. The history of bongo drumming can be traced to the Cuban music styles known as changüi and son. These styles first developed in eastern Cuba (Oriente province) in the late 19th century. Initially, the bongo had heads which were tacked and tuned with a heat source. By the 1940s, metal tuning lugs developed to facilitate easier tuning. Some of the first recordings of the bongo can be heard performed by the groups Sexteto Habanero, Sexteto Boloña and Septeto Nacional.

It is believed that bongos evolved from the Abakua drum trio 'Bonko' and its lead drum 'Bonko Enmiwewos'. These drums are still a fundamental part of the Abakua Religion in Cuba. If joined with a wooden peck in the middle, such drums would look much like the bongos we know today.

During the 1950-1960s, bongos were associated with the Beatniks who would use them to provide accents during pauses in poetry read in coffeehouses. The two small drums that make up Bongos are typically made of wood, metal, or composite materials, attached by a thick piece of wood. The drum head can be made of animal skin or it can be synthetic. Some *"bongoceros"* prefer the sound of X-ray Film as the head on the macho.

Bongo-like drums with ceramic bodies and goatskin or rawhide heads are found in Morocco where they are known as "tbila", as well as in Egypt and other Middle Eastern countries. They can sometimes be found accompanying flamenco and other traditional Spanish music, partially because of the Moorish influence in Spain. Ceramic bongos are more common in the Middle East and Asia than they are in South America; this is because wooden bongos were brought to Cuba during the slave trade. The basic rhythm on the Bongo is called: "Martillo" (Hammer); on the next page you will see a series of patterns used for Salsa as well as for Peruvian Music. Let's start with the basic *"Martillo"* rhythm.

Key:

T= Tip of the fingers	T= yemas de los dedos
TH= side of thumb	TH= costado del pulgar
O= open tone	O= tono abierto
M= muffled	M= apagado
S= Slap	S= tapado

{Track 26}

Now, let's look at *"El Medio Martillo"* or The Half Hammer, which consist on a conga like pattern which was widely used when the bands used 1 conga drum instead of 2. That pattern is commonly used now when you have a Conga player that is weak and threat the stability of the rhythm section.

{Track 27}

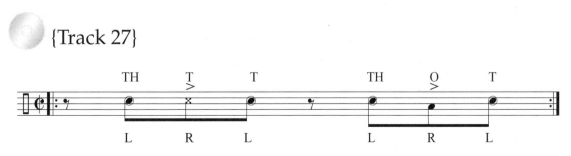

Now let's take a look at some variations for the *Martillo,* which can be used while performing at a Latin band.

Exercise (A) {Track 28}

Exercise (B) {Track 29}

Exercise (C) {Track 30}

Exercise (D) {Track 31}

Exercise (E)   {Track 32}

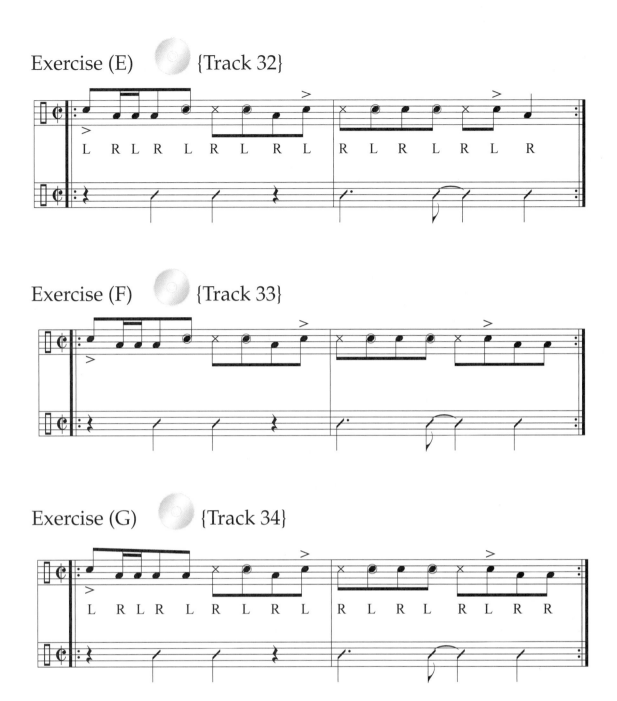

Exercise (F)   {Track 33}

Exercise (G)   {Track 34}

These are just few combinations which can be used at any time. We would recommend for you to listen to bongoceros like Anthony Carrillo, Johnny "Dandy" Rodriguez and many others. Create your own style and PLAY. Now, let's move on to contemporary techniques for hand drums. The first part is regarding Rudiments and from there we would move on to soloing.

Chapter 3

*"Applying Snare Drum Rudiments, Developing
Doubles and Soloing"*

Applying Snare rudiments on the Conga

{Track 35}

Once you have developed a good sound and mastered the tumbao you're ready to move on to something a little more difficult -- Applying and developing snare drum rudiments on the congas. In this chapter, we will discuss some of the basic snare drum rudiments and its application to the conga drums. We will not add doubles yet because in the next chapter we'll be discussing doubles and how to develop speed. *Rudiments*, as The New Merriam-Webster Dictionary describes it, are a basic skill -- Something that is not fully developed. However, for drumming is the starting point. It is something that starts basic but becomes very intense.

There are 25 basic *Rudiments* on snare drumming and are the first techniques drummers learn to develop. Once you master them you can use them infinitely. In this book, we will only discuss some of the basic *rudiments*; in our next edition we will add some other *rudiments* on a more advanced level. Let's start with our first *rudiment, "The Three Stroke Ruff"*.

Pearl Corporation roster at camp; pictured are Horacio "El Negro" Hernandez, Jose Rosa, Hector "Pocho" Neciosup, Dimas Sanchez and Glen Caruba

"The Three Stroke Ruff"

All short, Single Stroke Rolls are known as *"Ruffs"*. The rudiment in this lesson consists of three alternated strokes, the third of which is slapped. The rhythmic model of this rudiment, shown below is written in Half time or (2/2). Before we started reading music we learned these exercises by using vocal percussive language, which we are adding in to the exercise. For example: *"PA"* is the syllable for the right or left hand open slap, *"tu"* and *"ku"* are for the right or left hand open tone. Let's take a look to the first exercise.

 {Track 36}

The Three Stroke Ruff (accent on the third note)

Rhytmic Model: Play slow at first: increase speed gradually. Keep strict rhythm

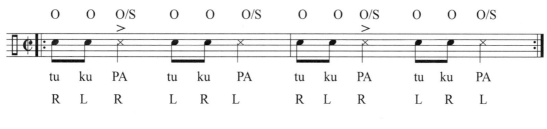

Key:
O/S = Open Slap
O = Open Tone

Remember to start this exercise slowly and gradually add speed to it in order to keep a strict rhythm. Now, we will add 2 more exercises with the accents on the second note and on the first note. Use your imagination to create your own exercises with this *rudiment*.

The Three Stroke Ruff (accent on the second note)

Rhytmic Model: Play slow at first: increase speed gradually. Keep strict rhythm

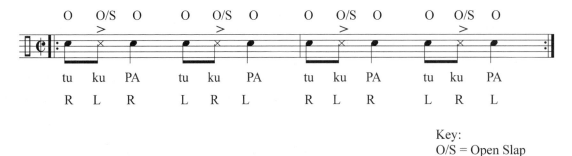

Key:
O/S = Open Slap
O   = Open Tone

The Three Stroke Ruff (slap on the first note)

Rhytmic Model: Play slow at first: increase speed gradually. Keep strict rhythm

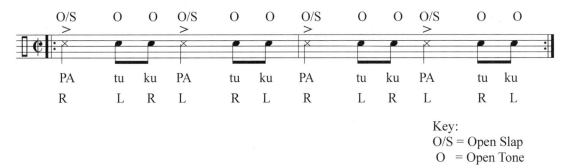

Key:
O/S = Open Slap
O   = Open Tone

These exercises should be practiced very slowly, at first and then gradually increasing the speed, always making sure that the sound is articulated. Let's move on to "The Four Stroke Ruff"

"The Four Stroke Ruff"

This rudiment consists of four alternated strokes, with a slap on the fourth stroke. When the left hand begins the *"Ruff"*, the right hand plays the *slap* and vice-versa. The rhythmic model of this rudiment is written in 6/8 time. There are six beats to each measure, the fifth and sixth of which are eight rests. The second example you will see is in 2/2, and we will add the vocal percussive language, *"TUKUTUPA"* to make it easier for people that do not read music. We suggest that you begin playing this *Ruff* at slow tempo at first, and then gradually increase the speed until the desired tempo is obtained.

{Track 37}

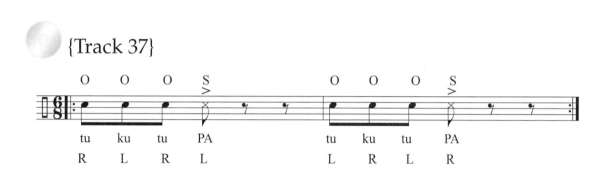

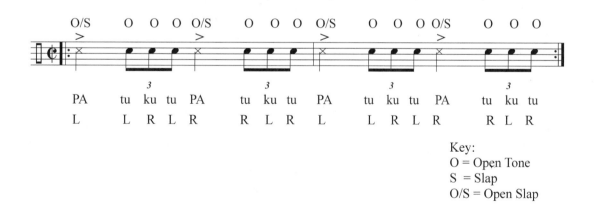

Key:
O = Open Tone
S = Slap
O/S = Open Slap

39

"The Five Stroke Ruff"

This rudiment consists of five alternated strokes, with an accent on the fifth stroke. The rhythmic model of this rudiment is written in 3/4 time. The second example you will see is in 2/2, and we will add the vocal percussive language, *"TUKUTUKUPA"* to make it easier for anyone who does not read music. We suggest that you begin playing this Ruff at a slow tempo at first, and then gradually increase the speed, until the desired tempo is obtained.

{Track 38}

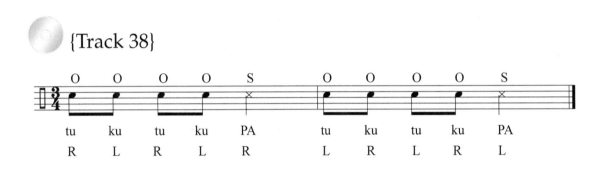

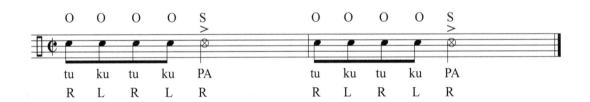

"The Flam"

This rudiment consists of a principle note (Large) preceded by a grace note (small note). In executing the *Flam*, the grace note is lightly tapped as "close" as possible to the principle (large) note. The important points to remember is that when executing a right hand Flam, the left hand leads while when playing a left hand Flam, the right hand leads. Old congueros used a lot of Flams on their soloing so Flam is basically a standard *"lick"* on solo performing. For this, we are using the syllable *"PLA"*. We recommend our students to this rudiment using a metronome starting on 60 to 120 Beats per second.

{Track 39}

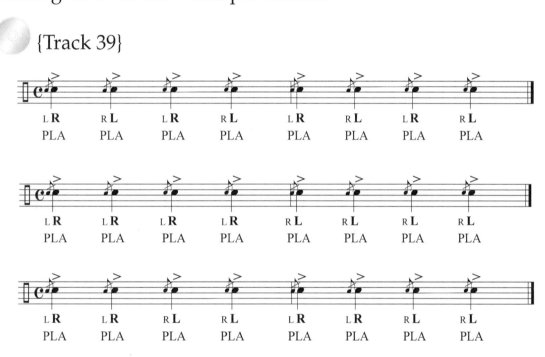

"The Flam Tap"

This *rudiment* is what its name implies – a *Flam* followed by a *"Tap"*. The grace note is played very lightly and the next two notes are accented with equal volume. We recommend that my students practice *Flams* using a metronome starting on 60 Beats per second up to 120 Beats per second.

"The Flam Accent"

This *rudiment* is what its name implies – a *Flam* followed by two *"Taps"*. The first note is accented while the other two notes are not. We will provide you with several examples of this *rudiment* with the accent placed on a different part of the rudiment. We always recommend our students to practice this rudiment using a metronome starting on 60 to 120 Beats per second.

Now, let's take a look at the same rudiment but with the accent on the second note.

Finally, we will look at this rudiment with the accent on the third note.

Remember, you can combine this exercise using different congas so that you can create your own exercise or solo performance. Let's now talk about doubles and how to develop speed on the congas.

Doubles – Developing Speed

This section will deal exclusively with all the aspects relating to doubles and how to develop a well balanced roll. We've been asked many times: "How can I develop the doubles on the conga? My answer is simply: Practice and Patience. "

Here is a very basic method to develop doubles. When you hit the conga typically the middle part of your hand hits the border of the conga (not the rim) and your finger hits close to the center of the drum. Normally the hand will bounce naturally on the drum. We think of it more like a snare drum. If you have never played snare drums then we would like to recommend for you to start listening, watching and learn about snare drums; pay close attention to marching drummers especially.

We try to visualize ourselves playing a snare drum and then listen to the conga drum for articulation. We'll explain it like this: *"Learning to do doubles is like learning a new language. It's hard in the beginning, you don't understand a word but with practice and determination you can dominate it."* The following exercises will help you develop doubles.

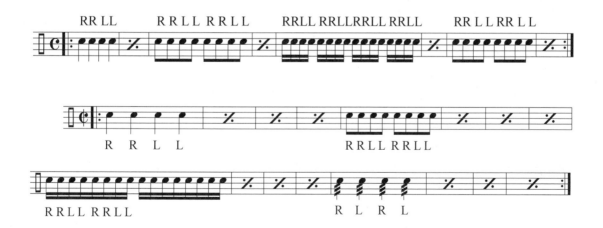

These are the main exercise to develop doubles. Practice this daily. Start at a slow tempo and eventually increase the tempo gradually. Let's do some rudiments that involve doubling: *Half Drag, Full Drag, 5 stroke roll, 9 stroke roll and paradiddles.* Enjoy…

"The Half Drag"

This rudiment should be practiced slowly. You can gradually build up the speed. We highly recommend practicing this rudiment using a towel on the conga drum. Now, let's take a look at the exercise.

R	L	L	R	L	L	R	L	L	R	L	L
L	R	R	L	R	R	L	R	R	L	R	R

Start practicing slow and gradually build up the speed

"The Full Drag"

A Full drag consists of a half drag, followed by a single accented stroke. The latter is made with the same hand that completes the half drag. This rudiment should be practiced slowly and increase the speed gradually.

LL R   R   RR L   L   LL R   R   RR L   L

RR L   L   LL R   R   RR L   L   LL R   R

"The Five stroke roll"

"The Nine stroke roll"

Slowly increase the speed while practicing this exercise.

"The Single Paradiddle"

This rudiment combines two single strokes with one double stroke.

These are just a few rudiments for you to use. Create your own combination and exercises with this.

Soloing –What's involved?

Soloing is an art. When you solo you want to draw a picture in which the audience can see and hear your masterpiece. A clear understanding along with inspiration is what makes a soloist construct a meaningful solo. A sequence which ends in a climax is an excellent solo or a sequence which creates a climax and it ends with a *decaying or entrega* (Spanish word for to give in) is another outstanding way of soloing.

In Latin music, the way you perform a solo is different from any other style. In this genre you want to use meaningful phrases based in *clave*, either *2/3 or 3/2, Son, Rumba, and 6/8*. That is why is necessary to practice phrasing in all claves to master the patterns in every clave. When we teach soloing we always start with quarter note phrasing, follow by eight note phrasing, then syncopated phrasing, and finally sixteenth phrasing. Don't forget the clave concept with every phrase.

One of the books we use is *"Syncopation"* by Ted Reed. After going through all the pages before the *syncopation* starts, we set up the metronome and go from page one (using the *clave* pattern on a *jam block* with my left foot). Once that is mastered then we continue with the *syncopation* part, playing one measure phrase, then two measures phrases, and finally through the whole page. Always at the end of a practice session we create our own combinations. We do the same thing with the triplet section in the book and we apply the 6/8 groove to it. Especially the accents have unlimited combinations because we can apply different sounds to them.

Transcribing solos is another good device to increment your solo vocabulary. This is something we are constantly doing, either mentally or written. We also ask our students to do the same. This way we are always getting new ideas and also getting involved in the development of how solos change from time to time. Transcriptions may include *solos "típicos"* (Spanish word for simple), melodic phrases from performers such as Carlos "Patato" Valdes, Tata Guines, Mongo Santamaria, Ray Barretto, etc. or contemporary style, which is a combination of melodic phrases with speed. You can hear contemporary soloing from "Master Congueros" such as Giovanni Hidalgo, Miguel Anga and Richie Flores.

In summary, solos involve everything you have at you disposition, from the basics to the most complicated rhythm. Solos can be performed in various styles depending on the effect the performer wants to achieve.

Jose, El Negro and Pocho.

Pocho and Jose at the Pearl Corporation booth at the Winter NAMM show, 2008.

How to apply rudiments into my solo?

The first conga Masters used very little rudiments. If you listen to their music you may hear a *flam, a ruff, a five stroke ruff*, and probably a *Paradiddle* but that was it. Often times they did not even knew that they were using them; it was the nature of transferring some rhythms that included those *rudiments*. Everything changed with one person, Giovanni Hidalgo; He took conga drumming to levels never seen before by *applying all the snare drum rudiments* in to the conga drumming.

He inspired the new generation of percussionists to study the entire snare drum rudiments and applying them to the congas. As a matter of fact, in our private lessons we teach all of our students to go through, "The Buddy Rich's Snare Drum rudiments", "150 Rudimental Solos by Charley Wilcoxon", and "Portraits in Rhythm by Anthony Cirone", all of these books are to be played on congas, using all dynamic levels. Of course, learning how to execute all of these books is part of the process. Next we would play each book with the clave using the wood block on the left foot and finally create your own solos based on the studied solos. Now let's take a look at the 3 congas independence exercises.

Exercises for Independence on Three Congas

Mongo Santamaria

Ramón "Mongo" Santamaría (April 7, 1922 in Havana, Cuba – February 1, 2003 in Miami, FL) was an Afro-Cuban Latin jazz percussionist. He is most famous for being the composer of the jazz standard "Afro Blue," recorded by John Coltrane among others. In 1950 he moved to New York where he played with Perez Prado, Tito Puente, Cal Tjader, Fania All Stars, etc. He was an integral figure in the fusion of Afro-Cuban rhythms with R&B and soul, paving the way for the boogaloo era of the late 1960s. His 1963 hit rendition of Herbie Hancock's "Watermelon Man" was inducted into the Grammy Hall of Fame in 1998.

Santamaria inspired the stage name of Japanese actor Yusuke Santamaria. Additionally, his name is used as a pun in the film Blazing Saddles. When the character of Mongo entered a scene, a character cried, "Mongo! Santa Maria!".

He is buried in Woodlawn Park Cemetery and Mausoleum (now Caballero Rivero Woodlawn Park North Cemetery and Mausoleum) in Miami, Florida.

Chapter 4

"Afro-Caribbean Rhythms"

Mambo and Cha-Cha

P T S P T P O O O   P T S P T P O O

Guajira

P T S P T P O O O   P T S P T P O T

Bolero

P T S T P O O O   P T S T P O O O

Guaguanco 3-2 Rumba Clave

R L L R L L R L R L R L L R L L R L

T P T B P T O T   O P T O P T O T

Guaguanco (3 Congas)

Playing 3-2 clave at the same time

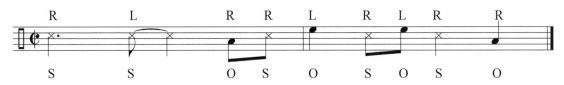

R   L   R R L R L R   R

S   S   O S O S O S   O

Songo

Songo
ver 2

Songo
Van Van Style

Songo
Variation by Jose Rosa

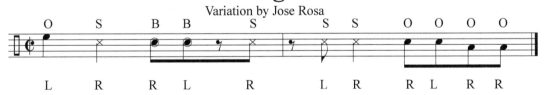

Bomba Sica

{Tracks 52/53}

Bomba Cuembe

Bomba Holandes

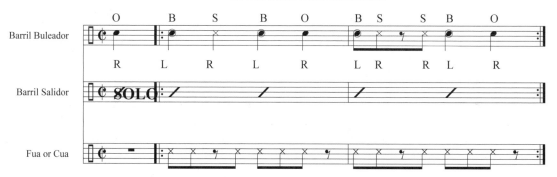

{Tracks 54/55}

Plena

(2 Congas) ver 1.

(3 Congas) ver 1.

54

Orisa
Papo Pepin Style

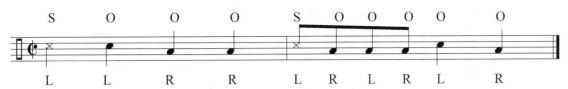

{Tracks 56/57}

Orisa - Puerto Rico
This pattern can be used in Soca

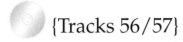

Orisa
ver 2.

{Tracks 58/59}

Mozambique

{Tracks 60/61}

Rumba Columbia

{Tracks 62/63}

Pilon

{Tracks 64/65}

Cumbia

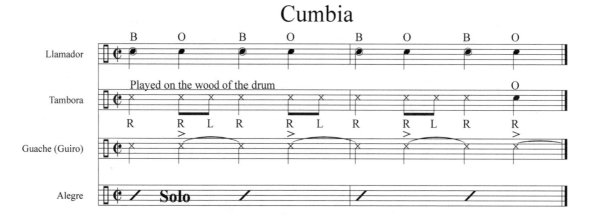

Abakua for 3 congas

Columbia

David Lamole
3 Congas

Merengue

Merengue a lo Maco

Tumbao en 7

Tumbao en 9

American Pop-Rock

Giovanni Hidalgo
(Pictured here with Jose Rosa)

His grandfather had also been a musician as well as his father, José Manuel Hidalgo "Mañengue", who was a renowned conga player. Therefore, Hidalgo was raised in a household surrounded by drums, bongos, congas and timbales. As a young child he practiced and developed his speed and playing skills on the conga and on the other instruments in his house. Hidalgo would drum a tune with sticks and then play the same tune with his hands.

Hidalgo auditioned and was hired by the Batacumbele Band in 1980. In 1981, he traveled with the band to Cuba where he met a musician by the name of José Luis Quintana "Changuito". Together they were able to create a unique style of rhythm and ushered in a new musical era in Latin music.

In 1985, Hidalgo was performing with Eddie Palmieri at The Village Gate in New York City, when the legendary jazz musician Dizzy Gillespie walked in and listened to Hidalgo play. He was so impressed with Hidalgo that he told him that someday in the future they must get together and play—this happened in 1988 when Hidalgo joined the Dizzy Gillespie United Nations Jazz Orchestra. He is widely regarded as the greatest living conga player.

Chapter 5

"La Mano Secreta and Independence Exercises"

La Mano Secreta "Secret Hand" Exercise

Left Hand Patterns:
A)   P T P T P T P T
B)   P T T T P T T T   C)   P T T T T T T T

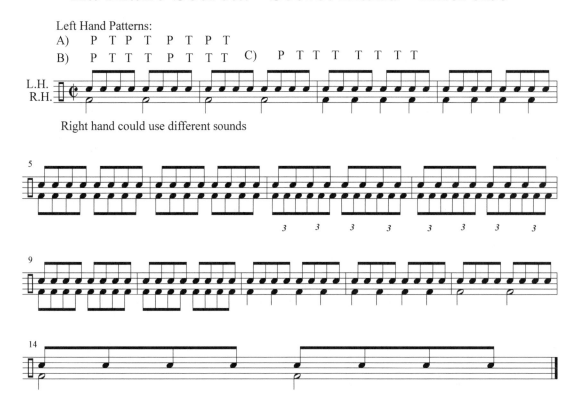

Right hand could use different sounds

Exercises in 6/8

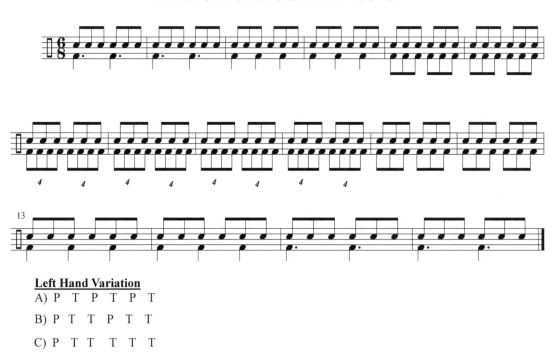

Left Hand Variation

A) P T P T P T

B) P T T P T T

C) P T T T T T

Independence Exercises

This is a series of exercises for independence, the best way to study this exercises is by switching hands. Play the clave with the Left hand and then play it with the right hand.

Exercise (A)

Exercise (B)

Exercise (C)

Exercise (D)

Exercise (E)

Exercise (F)

Exercise (G)

Exercise (H)

Exercise (I)

Exercise (J)

Exercise (K)

Now, let's do some exercises using 6/8 and 5/8 time measures. The first 9 exercises will develop you on a variation of Abakua and 5/8 Exercise is just for fun. You will have noticed that the clave is written on the top now, please don't get confused. You can start the exercise playing either the Left or right hand on the clave. Enjoy

Exercise (A)

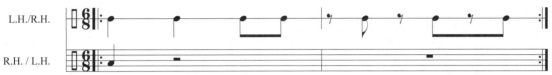

Exercise (B)

Exercise (C)

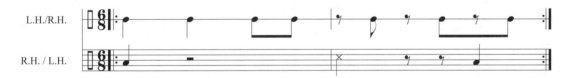

Exercise (D)

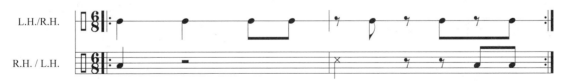

Exercise (E)

Exercise (F)

Exercise (G)

Exercise (H)

Exercise (I)

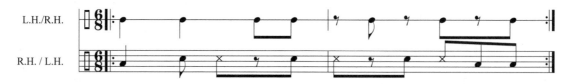

Exercise (J)

Exercise (K)

Exercise (L)

Exercise (M)

Exercise (N)

Exercise (O)

Exercise (P)

With this exercise we are closing this chapter; I hope you had enjoyed this chapter. Create your own exercises and practice independence with many other rhythms.

Conclusion {Track 68}

In summary, we have learned all basic aspects of modern hand drumming techniques. We hope this book has been a blessing for you and we pray that God will give you the wisdom and understanding that you need to develop musically. If you are just a beginning musician, keep doing the work, practice, practice, practice and create your own style. If you are a professional musician, keep doing the work. We want to wish you the best of luck in this business and remember that if you don't understand something we are always available for private and/or group lessons.

God Bless you,

José Rosa &
Héctor "Pocho" Neciosup

How to Contact Us

Hector and Jose are available for clinics, private and group lessons, for more information contact us through our web-sites located at:

Our Summer Camp:
http://www.contemporarypercussion.com

Our Main Website:
http://www.clmeducators.com

1 on 1 ONLINE PRIVATE LESSON
NOW AVAILABLE
Contact us for more information about
price and hardware requirements

Visit our "MY SPACE" pages located at:
Héctor "Pocho" Neciosup – www.myspace.com/pochoneciosup
José Rosa - www.myspace.com/josemrosa

Credits

Executive Producers: Ron Middlebrook, Jose Rosa and Hector "Pocho" Neciosup for CenterStream Publishing

Music Producers and arrangers: Jose Rosa and Hector "Pocho" Neciosup

Audio Production: Contemporary Latin Music Educators for CenterStream Publishing

Audio Engineers: José Rosa, Héctor "Pocho" Neciosup

Mastering: CLM Productions

Music Performed by: "Tinya" - Featuring Héctor "Pocho" Neciosup – Conga Solo, Timbales, Güiro, Cua. And José Rosa – Conga Solo, Bongo and Bongo Cowbell.

Brief Discography

This is just a brief list for your information, search for these titles and buy the CD's this is the best tool your career

Chano Pozo

1-   Cuban Rhythms-
       Release Date: 08/31/1999 Label: World Of Music
       UPC: 793515256429

2-   Legendary Sessions 1947-1953
       Release Date: 11/16/2004 Label: Tumbao Cuban Classix
       UPC: 842732811017

3-   Tambor de Cuba – Unknown, you can search for it at Amazon.com

4-   Manteca-
       Release Date: 11/16/2004, Label: Tumbao Cuban Classix
       UPC: 8427328111027

Carlos "Patato" Valdez

1-   Patato & Totico (1968) Remastered;
2-   El Hombre (2004)
3-   Legend Of Cuban Percussion (2000)
4-   The Conga Kings

Mongo Santamaria

1-   Afro Blue: The Picante Collection (1997)
2-   Afro Roots
3-   Afro-Indio
4-   Arriba!
5-   At The Black Hawk
6-   Blackout
7-   Brazilian Sunset (1996)
8-   Espiritu Libre (2007)
9-   Feelin' Alright (1970)
10-   Free Spirit
11-   Fuego
12-   Greatest Hits (1987)
13-   Willie Bobo / Mongo Santamaria / Cal Tjader - Latino!
14-   Live At Jazz Alley (1990)
15-   Mongo '70/Mongo At Montreax (1970)
16-   Mongo At Montreux

17-   Mongo At The Village Gate (1963)
18-   Mongo Explodes/Watermelon Man
19-   **Mongo Introduces La Lupe**
20-   **Mongo Returns (1995)**
21-   Mongo's Way/Up From The Roots (1971)
22-   Montreux Heat (2003)
23-   Mucho Mongo (2001)
24-   Our Man In Havana (1960)
25-   Sabroso!
26-   Skin On Skin: Mongo Santamaria Anthology 1958-1995 (1999)
27-   Sofrito
28-   Summertime (1980)
29-   Up From Roots
30-   Watermelon Man (1963)
31-   Watermelon Man: B.O. Santamaria, Mongo

Ray Barretto

1-   Acid Remastered
2-   Aqui Se Puede (1987) Remastered
3-   Barretto (1975)
4-   Remastered
5-   Barretto Power Remastered
6-   Carnaval (1962)
7-   Celia-Ray-Adalberto-Tremendo Trio! (1992) Remastered
8-   Giant Force (1980) Remastered
9-   Greatest Hits (2007) Remastered
10-   Hard Hands Remastered
11-   Homage To Art Blakey (2003)
12-   Hot Hands (2003)
13-   Indestructible
14-   Irresistible Remastered
15-   Latin Soul Man (2007)
16-   Live In Puerto Rico (2006) Holland
17-   Man And His Music: The Essential Ray Barretto (2007) Remastered
18-   Message (2007) Remastered
19-   Que Viva La Musica (2006) Remastered
20-   Rhythm Of Life
21-   Rican/Struction Remastered
22-   Soy Dichoso Remastered
23-   Standards Rican-Ditioned (2006)
24-   Time Was...Time Is (2005)
25-   Together Remastered
26-   Tomorrow: Live (1976)
27-   Trancedance (2001)

Did you like this book? If so,
check out Beyond "The Secret Hand"

BEYOND "THE SECRET HAND"
A Comprehensive Guide for Hand Drummers
by Héctor "Poncho" Neciosup & José Rosa, Foreword by Glen Caruba
In Spanish & English
This book/CD pack is designed for the hand drummer that is eager to step up to the next level in performance. You will develop a good sound by incorporating strengthening exercises coupled with various techniques to develop strength, speed, independence, and control. Practical exercises for coordination and independence are included to help you increase your level of performance. The CD includes a performance track by Poncho and José.
00001175 Book/CD Pack...$19.95

P.O. Box 17878 - Anaheim Hills, CA 92817
(714) 779-9390   www.centerstream-usa.com